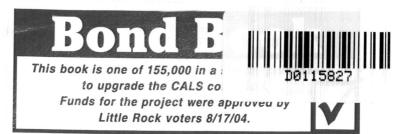

THE REPUBLIC OF POETRY

OTHER BOOKS BY MARTÍN ESPADA

POETRY

Alabanza: New and Selected Poems (1982–2002)

A Mayan Astronomer in Hell's Kitchen

Imagine the Angels of Bread

City of Coughing and Dead Radiators

Rebellion is the Circle of a Lover's Hands

Trumpets from the Islands of Their Eviction

The Immigrant Iceboy's Bolero

TRANSLATION

The Blood That Keeps Singing: Selected Poems of Clemente Soto Vélez
(with Camilo Pérez-Bustillo)

EDITOR

El Coro: A Chorus of Latino and Latina Poetry

Poetry Like Bread: Poets of the Political Imagination from Curbstone Press

ESSAYS

Zapata's Disciple

Auf der Suche nach la Revolución
(essays and poems in German translation)

AUDIOBOOK

Now the Dead will Dance the Mambo

THE REPUBLIC OF POETRY

MARTÍN ESPADA

W. W. NORTON & COMPANY

NEW YORK   LONDON

For information about permission to reproduce selections from this book, write to
Permissions, W. W. Norton & Company, Inc., 500 Fifth Avenue, New York, NY 10110

Manufacturing by Courier Westford
Book design by Lovedog Studio
Production manager: Anna Oler

Library of Congress Cataloging-in-Publication Data

Espada, Martín, 1957–
The republic of poetry / Martin Espada. — 1st ed.
p. cm.
Poems.
ISBN-13: 978-0-393-06256-4 (hardcover)
ISBN-10: 0-393-06256-2 (hardcover)
I. Title.
PS3555.S53R47 2006
811'.54—dc22

2006013008

W. W. Norton & Company, Inc., 500 Fifth Avenue, New York, N.Y. 10110
www.wwnorton.com

W. W. Norton & Company Ltd., Castle House, 75/76 Wells Street, London W1T 3QT

1 2 3 4 5 6 7 8 9 0

This book is dedicated to Darío

Contents

Acknowledgments xi

I. THE REPUBLIC OF POETRY

THE REPUBLIC OF POETRY 3

NOT HERE 5

SOMETHING ESCAPES THE BONFIRE 8

THE SOLDIERS IN THE GARDEN 12

BLACK ISLANDS 14

RAIN WITHOUT RAIN 15

NOT PAINT AND WOOD 18

SONNET IN PRAISE OF JAIVA PIE 19

I HAVE AN EEL IN MY HEART 20

CITY OF GLASS 22

AN ADMIRER OF GENERAL PINOCHET WRITES
TO THE WEB SITE OF GENERAL PINOCHET TO
WISH GENERAL PINOCHET A HAPPY BIRTHDAY 24

GENERAL PINOCHET AT THE BOOKSTORE 25

II. THE POET'S COAT

The Poet's Coat   29

You Got a Song, Man   31

The Face on the Envelope   34

Not Words but Hands   36

Stone Hammered to Gravel   37

Rules for Captain Ahab's Provincetown Poetry Workshop   40

Advice to Young Poets   41

III. THE WEATHER-BEATEN FACE

Return   45

Blues for the Soldiers Who Told You   46

The God of the Weather-Beaten Face   48

Between the Rockets and the Songs   51

To the Burmese Albino Python Living in the Next Room   52

Why My Bones Hate the Ice   55

The Caves of Camuy   57

Notes on the Poems   59

Acknowledgments

These poems have appeared or will appear in the following publications, to whose editors grateful acknowledgment is made:

The Bloomsbury Review: "Black Islands," "The Republic of Poetry"

Dance the Guns to Silence: 100 Poems for Ken Saro-Wiwa: "The Soldiers in the Garden"

Hanging Loose: "An Admirer of General Pinochet Writes to the Web Site of General Pinochet to Wish General Pinochet a Happy Birthday," "Between the Rockets and the Songs," "Blues for the Soldiers Who Told You," "To the Burmese Albino Python in the Next Room," "The God of the Weather-Beaten Face"

Illuminations: "Stone Hammered to Gravel"

In The Grove: "Rules for Captain Ahab's Provinceton Poetry Workshop," "Advice to Young Poets," "I Have an Eel in My Heart"

The Massachusetts Review: "You Got a Song, Man"

Meena: A Bilingual Journal of Arts and Letters: "Why My Bones Hate the Ice"

The New Yorker: "City of Glass," "Return"

Peacework: "General Pinochet at the Bookstore"

Ploughshares: "The Poet's Coat"

The Progressive: "Not Here"

Rattapallax: "City of Glass," "General Pinochet at the Bookstore," "Not Here," "Rain Without Rain," "Something Escapes the Bonfire," "Sonnet in Praise of Jaiva Pie"

Excerpt from "Pastoral of Chile" (IX) from *Anteparadise* by Raúl Zurita, translated by Jack Schmitt, copyright © 1986 by the Regents of the University of California. Reprinted by permission of the University of California Press.

Many thanks to the following individuals and organizations: to Jack Agüeros, for his translations of Julia de Burgos and his research on her life; to Doug Anderson and the other veteran writers of the Joiner Center; to María Luisa Arroyo, for proofreading; to Chris Brandt and the Medicine Show Theatre, for adapting three of the Chile poems for the stage in their production, *The Republic of Poetry;* to Ram Devineni, Bob Madey, Rodrigo Rojas, and José Ignacio Silva, for making the visit to Chile possible and memorable; to Ariel Dorfman, for reading the Chile poems; to Katherine and Klemente Gilbert-Espada, my wife and son; to George Evans, for his help with images of Marfa, Texas; to Frances Goldin, my heroic agent; to Sam Hamill and Poets Against War, for posting two of these poems on their Web site (poetsagainstwar.net), and for all their good work; to Joan Jara, for sharing her story with me at Estadio Víctor Jara; to Yusef Komunyakaa and Nathalie Handal, the poets who joined me on the journey to Neruda's Chile; to Oscar Sarmiento, for translating the Chile poems into Spanish; to the John Simon Guggenheim Memorial Foundation and the AE Ventures Foundation, for their support; to compañero Raúl Zurita, for the walk at La Moneda; and to the Acentos/LouderArts crew (Oscar, Rich, Fish, Jessica, Elial, Roger, y Lynne). See also "Notes on the Poems."

I.

THE REPUBLIC OF POETRY

THE REPUBLIC OF POETRY
for Chile

In the republic of poetry,
a train full of poets
rolls south in the rain
as plum trees rock
and horses kick the air,
and village bands
parade down the aisle
with trumpets, with bowler hats,
followed by the president
of the republic,
shaking every hand.

In the republic of poetry,
monks print verses about the night
on boxes of monastery chocolate,
kitchens in restaurants
use odes for recipes
from eel to artichoke,
and poets eat for free.

In the republic of poetry,
poets read to the baboons
at the zoo, and all the primates,
poets and baboons alike, scream for joy.

In the republic of poetry,
poets rent a helicopter
to bombard the national palace
with poems on bookmarks,
and everyone in the courtyard
rushes to grab a poem
fluttering from the sky,
blinded by weeping.

In the republic of poetry,
the guard at the airport
will not allow you to leave the country
until you declaim a poem for her
and she says *Ah! Beautiful.*

NOT HERE

for Raúl Zurita
Santiago de Chile, July 2004

The other poets tell me he tried to blind himself,
taped his eyelids and splashed his face with ammonia.

What Zurita saw gnawed like a parasite at the muscles in his eyes:
Chile's warships invaded the harbor of Valparaíso
and subversives staggered at gunpoint
through the city of hills down to the dock.
Only the water knows how many
faded away like black boots tossed into a black sea,
or dangled from the masts, beaten by knuckles and rain
into scarecrows the seagulls would pluck.

September 11, 1973: Zurita's heart
crashed deep in the ribs of a navy ship.
The officer in charge of interrogation
shook the poet's papers and fumed: *This is not poetry.*
The other poets tell me: *Electricity was involved.*

Seven years later, Zurita blinked
to save his eyes, and wrote:
in the name of our love let even
the steel-toed boots
that kicked us be loved

5

and those who mocking us said
"Do a little dance for us" and put out their cigarettes
on our arms so we would dance for them
for our love's sake, for that alone,
let them now dance.

Today we walk through the courtyard
of the presidential palace.
The fountain speaks in the water's tongue;
the fountain of smoke is gone.
The bombers that boomed across this sky
left no fingerprints in the clouds
when they dropped their rockets,
twisting the rails of the balcony like licorice.
Today Allende is white marble outside the palace,
mute as a martyr, without a hand free to wave
from the balcony, without a voice to crackle
his last words in the radio air.

Zurita says: *After the bombing, after the coup,*
no one could stand here to look at the ruins.
If you did, you were suspect. Did you grieve for Allende?
They grieved, heads down, hands in pockets, moving along,
glancing up, a blackened balcony in the corner of the eye.
Zurita knows what the water knows,
what the sky will not confess even to the gods
who switch the electricity on, off, then on again.
Zurita's beard is forged in gray, the steel of a navy ship.

He lights a cigarette for those who would see the ruins
where the ruins have been swept away.

I am the one navigating the night without stars.
On or around the night of September 11, 1973,
at the age of sixteen,
I was vandalizing a golf course in the rain,
fishtailing my car through the mud on the ninth hole
as beer cans rolled under my feet.
Ten miles away, at the White House,
the plotters were pleased; the coup
was a world in miniature they painted by hand,
a train with real smoke and bells
circling the track in the basement.
The rest of us drank too much, drove too fast,
as the radio told us what happened
on the other side of the world
and the windshield wipers said
not here, not here, not here.

SOMETHING ESCAPES THE BONFIRE

for Víctor and Joan Jara

I. Because We Will Never Die: June 1969

Víctor sang his peasant's prayer:
Levántate, y mírate las manos.
Stand up and look at your hands,
gloved in hard skin, the hands of Víctor's father
petrified into fists steering the plow.
Estadio Chile cheered, delirious as a man
who knows he has plowed his last field
for someone else, who hears a song telling him
what he knows with the back of his neck.

Joan, the dancer, who twirled before crowds
at the same shantytowns where Víctor sang,
leaned forward in her seat to hear it:
First Prize at the New Song festival for Víctor Jara.
These are the nights we do not sleep
because we will never die.
How then could he squint into the dark,
somewhere beyond the back row, raise his guitar,
and sing: *We'll go together, united by blood,*
now and in the hour of our death. Amen.

II. *The Man with All the Guns: September 1973*

The coup came, and soldiers whipped the enemies of the state,
hands on head and single file, through the stadium gates.
Condemned faces bled their light in the halls
of Estadio Chile. The light floats there still.
The killers had their light too, spectral cigarettes
glimmering in every corridor, especially the Prince,
or so the prisoners called the blond officer
who smiled at his work as if churches sang in his head.

When Víctor slipped into the hallway,
away from thousands gripping knees to chest
as they awaited the cigarette in the neck
or stared back at the staring machine guns,
he met the Prince, who must have heard singing in his head,
since he recognized the singer's face, strummed the air
and slashed a finger across his throat.
The Prince smiled like a man with all the guns.

Later, when the other prisoners realized
there were no wings on their shoulders
to fly them from the firing squad,
Víctor sang *"Venceremos,"* we will win,
and the banned anthem lifted shoulders
as the Prince's face reddened in a scream.

If his own scream could not quiet the song
pulsing through the veins in his head,
reasoned the Prince, then the machine guns would.

III. If Only Víctor: July 2004

Crack the face of every clock at Estadio Chile.
In this place, thirty-one years are measured
by Víctor's last breath. A moment,
as in *momento*, the last word of the last canto
he wrote before the bullets swarmed
into the honeycomb of his lungs.

Her eyes still burn. Her tongue still freezes.
Again for Joan the helicopters roar,
military music drums across the dial,
soldiers rifle-butt women in the bread line.
Again she finds her husband's body in the morgue
amid the corpses piled like laundry
and lifts his dangling fractured hands in hers
as if to begin a waltz.

Yes, now they have named the stadium where he was killed for him;
yes, his words flow in stone across the wall of the lobby;
yes, there are Chinese acrobats tumbling here tonight;
yet she would rip away the sign flourishing his name,
hammer down the wall of his words
and scatter the acrobats into the streets

if only Víctor would walk into the room
to finish their argument about why
he moved so slowly in the morning
that he almost always made her late for class.

IV. Something Escapes the Bonfire: July 2004

South of Santiago, far from Estadio Víctor Jara,
under a tent where the spikes of rain rattle off the canvas,
a boy and girl born years after the coup
lean across a chair onstage to fill their eyes with each other's faces.
The tape rumbles, and Víctor's voice
spirals delicate as burnt paper to the ceiling,
singing of a lover's silence to the dancers
who uncurl the tendrils of their bodies.

Something escapes the bonfire
where the generals warm their hands,
embers from burnt paper, buried tapes,
voices teeming in the silence
like the invisible creatures in a glass of water,
how a dancer spins to the music in her head,
alone but for the tingle of fingertips at her elbow.

THE SOLDIERS IN THE GARDEN

Isla Negra, Chile, September 1973

After the coup,
the soldiers appeared
in Neruda's garden one night,
raising lanterns to interrogate the trees,
cursing at the rocks that tripped them.
From the bedroom window
they could have been
the conquistadores of drowned galleons,
back from the sea to finish
plundering the coast.

The poet was dying;
cancer flashed through his body
and left him rolling in the bed to kill the flames.
Still, when the lieutenant stormed upstairs,
Neruda faced him and said:
There is only one danger for you here: poetry.
The lieutenant brought his helmet to his chest,
apologized to señor Neruda
and squeezed himself back down the stairs.
The lanterns dissolved one by one from the trees.

For thirty years
we have been searching
for another incantation
to make the soldiers
vanish from the garden.

BLACK ISLANDS

for Darío

At Isla Negra,
between Neruda's tomb
and the anchor in the garden,
a man with stonecutter's hands
lifted up his boy of five
so the boy's eyes could search mine.
The boy's eyes were black olives.
Son, the father said, *this is a poet,*
like Pablo Neruda.
The boy's eyes were black glass.
My son is called Darío,
for the poet of Nicaragua,
the father said.
The boy's eyes were black stones.
The boy said nothing,
searching my face for poetry,
searching my eyes for his own eyes.
The boy's eyes were black islands.

RAIN WITHOUT RAIN

Isla Negra, Chile, July 2004

The celebration of a century since Neruda's birth
brings pilgrims by the thousands to his house,
fingering the rust off the locomotive in his garden,
shouting Whitman in Spanish over the sea,
loading their shoes with Isla Negra sand
amid the red banners along the beach,
men on horseback, a chorus of schoolgirls,
bamboo flutes from the south.

Yet there is rain without rain in the air.
In the horseshoe path of the poet's tomb
they walk, lips sewn up by the seamstress grief,
faces of the disappeared on signs strung
around their necks: *Name. Date. Political Execution.*
The faces of the missing in snapshots are pins
brilliant in the sky, long after their bodies
float away to another cosmos.
Some wore jackets and ties for the journey;
one blinked with the camera's flash, shutting his eyes forever.

Thirty years ago the dictator
flicked a white-gloved hand
and the disappeared were gone:

Tape across the eyes, wires clamped to toes and genitals,
rats in the anus, a human ear in the soup.
Executioners hid their bones away
like dogs pawing at the soil.

Now the circle speaks at the poet's tomb:
my brother, my sister, my uncle, my cousin.
Give us the bones for the coffin,
give us the coffin for the grave,
give us the grave for the gravestone,
give us the gravestone so we can sleep.
Fingertips tilt the faces of the dead,
the family nose like three cloves of garlic,
mouth bent in a grin mysterious as a magician's spoon.

A girl, ten years old, wears the picture of a boy,
also ten, wandered off long ago into the dictator's carnival.
This is my uncle, she says. *I never met him.*
Then she recites Neruda, too softly, too quickly,
because her uncle should be there
to steer her shoulder and whisper: *Louder. Slower.*

How the *desaparecidos* on this day
burst from the sand at Isla Negra,
how they are born from the black petals of the rocks,
how they wade from a sea far away
where their bones glow with the light of blind fish.

At the tomb, a woman silent all along
steps from the circle and says:
I want to sing. Neruda. Poem Twenty.
Then she climbs atop the tomb and sings:
Tonight I can write the saddest verses.

NOT PAINT AND WOOD

I saw her at Neruda's house,
carved a century ago
to keep vigil over the waves
from the prow of a ship,
with great brown eyes
and hair in a whirl,
now hovering silently
above the poet's table.

That night in the bar
she appeared at my elbow,
the same eyes, the same hair,
not paint and wood but flesh.
He likes for me to be still,
she grinned. *I don't like to be still.*
I want to climb the steps
at Macchu Picchu.
I want to talk about poetry all night.
I want more wine.

SONNET IN PRAISE OF JAIVA PIE

Better than the crab sparring
like a brave featherweight
in the fisherman's hand
or the cook's eye,

better than the long table of anticipation
overlooking the sea at Isla Negra,
better than the fork happy
as a buccaneer's shovel over the treasure,

better than the benediction
of bread crumbs or the holy oil of butter,
better than the steam steaming from the bowl
are the two red claws poking through the crust,

one waving *hello*,
the other waving *good-bye.*

I HAVE AN EEL IN MY HEART

I have an eel in my heart,
wriggling through every chamber,
popping up from every shipwreck
to startle the divers scavenging down there,
a conger eel from the seas of Chile
amazing the doctors
who spread their hands far apart
to show the other doctors
what they found on the X-rays.

I have an eel in my heart,
fried, fried, fried
from the tables of Chile,
coiling in my chest,
squeezing the red muscle
till I bellow for an all-eel diet.

I have an eel in my heart,
saluted with another glass of wine
by the poets of Chile
who slam the table and argue:
Is this the mermaid with bulging eyes and needle teeth
celebrated in song two hundred years ago
by the lonely pirates of Valparaíso?

I have an eel in my heart.
I want to smuggle the serpent home from Chile,
a guitar case on the Santiago flight
reeking so radiantly
not even the Mormon missionaries
would speak to me.
Oh eel,
Neruda stewed you in an ode,
the Japanese sushi you with a perfect knife,
but I would waltz with you in my kitchen
before I do to you what your cousin the worm
finally does to us all.

CITY OF GLASS

for Pablo Neruda and Matilde Urrutia
La Chascona, Santiago de Chile

The poet's house was a city of glass:
cranberry glass, milk glass, carnival glass,
red and green goblets row after row,
black luster of wine in bottles,
ships in bottles, zoo of bottles,
rooster, horse, monkey, fish,
heartbeat of clocks tapping against crystal,
windows illuminated by the white Andes,
observatory of glass over Santiago.

When the poet died,
they brought his coffin to the city of glass.
There was no door: the door was a thousand daggers,
beyond the door an ancient world in ruins,
glass now arrowheads, axes, pottery shards, dust.
There were no windows: fingers of air
reached for glass like a missing lover's face.
There was no zoo: the bottles were half-moons
and quarter-moons, horse and monkey
eviscerated with every clock, with every lamp.
Bootprints spun in a lunatic tango across the floor.

The poet's widow said, *We will not sweep the glass.*
His wake is here. Reporters, photographers,
intellectuals, ambassadors stepped across the glass
cracking like a frozen lake, and soldiers too,
who sacked the city of glass,
returned to speak for their general,
three days of official mourning
announced at the end of the third day.

In Chile, a river of glass bubbled, cooled,
hardened, and rose in sheets, only to crash and rise again.
One day, years later, the soldiers wheeled around
to find themselves in a city of glass.
Their rifles turned to carnival glass;
bullets dissolved, glittering, in their hands.
From the poet's zoo they heard monkeys cry;
from the poet's observatory they heard
poem after poem like a call to prayer.
The general's tongue burned with slivers
invisible to the eye. The general's tongue
was the color of cranberry glass.

AN ADMIRER OF GENERAL PINOCHET WRITES TO THE WEB SITE OF GENERAL PINOCHET TO WISH GENERAL PINOCHET A HAPPY BIRTHDAY

To our Leader, Captain General Don Augusto Pinochet Ugarte:

It is my high honor to send you birthday greetings.
On this most special of days, turn a deaf ear to the traitors
and enjoy the festivities with a clean conscience.
I don't know how long the undesirables of the left
will keep on harassing the LIBERATOR OF CHILE.
They are everywhere: television, books,
magazines, newspapers, as if they could
change history, but no my Great General!
They are beasts who scavenge by night
and turn into white doves by day.

Many little kisses . . .

GENERAL PINOCHET AT THE BOOKSTORE
Santiago, Chile, July 2004

The general's limo parked at the corner of San Diego street
and his bodyguards escorted him to the bookstore
called La Oportunidad, so he could browse
for rare works of history.

There were no bloody fingerprints left on the pages.
No books turned to ash at his touch.
He did not track the soil of mass graves on his shoes,
nor did his eyes glow red with a demon's heat.

Worse: His hands were scrubbed, and his eyes were blue,
and the dementia that raged in his head like a demon,
making the general's trial impossible, had disappeared.

Desaparecido: like thousands dead but not dead,
as the crowd reminded the general,
gathered outside the bookstore to jeer
when he scurried away with his bodyguards,
so much smaller in person.

II

THE POET'S COAT

THE POET'S COAT

for Jeff Male (1946–2003)

When I cough, people duck away,
afraid of the coal miner's disease,
the imagined eruption of blood
down the chin. In the emergency room
the doctor gestures at the X-ray
where the lung crumples like a tossed poem.

You heard me cough, slipped off your coat
and draped it with ceremony across my shoulders,
so I became the king of rain and wind.
Keep it, you said. *You are my teacher.*
I kept it, a trench coat with its own film noir detective swagger.

The war in Viet Nam snaked rivers of burning sampans
through your brain, but still your hands
filled with poems gleaming like fish.
The highways of Virginia sent Confederate ghost-patrols
to hang you in dreams, a Black man with too many books,
but still you tugged the collar of your coat around my neck.

Now you are dead, your heart throbbing too fast
for the doctors at the veterans' hospital to keep the beat,
their pill bottles rattling, maracas in a mambo for the doomed.

On the night of your memorial service in Boston,
I wore your coat in a storm along the Florida shoreline.
The wind stung my face with sand, and with every slap
I remembered your ashes; with every salvo of arrows
in the rain your coat became the armor of a samurai.
On the beach I found the skeleton of a blowfish,
his spikes and leopard skin eaten away by the conqueror salt.
Your coat banished the conqueror back into the sea.

Soon your ashes fly to the veterans' cemetery at Arlington,
where once a Confederate general
would have counted you among his mules and pigs.
This poet's coat is your last poem.
I want to write a poem like this coat,
with buttons and pockets and green cloth,
a poem useful as a coat to a coughing man.
Teach me.

You Got a Song, Man

for Robert Creeley (1926–2005)

You told me the son of Acton's town nurse
would never cross the border
into Concord, where the Revolution
left great houses standing on Main Street.
Yet we crossed into Concord, walking
through Sleepy Hollow Cemetery
to greet Thoreau, his stone
stamped with the word *Henry*
jutting like a gray thumbnail
down the path from Emerson
and his boulder of granite.
We remembered Henry's night in jail,
refusing tax for the Mexican War,
and I could see you hunched with him,
loaning Henry a cigarette, explaining
the perpetual wink of your eye
lost after the windshield
burst in your boyhood face.
When Emerson arrived
to ask what you and Henry
were doing in there, you would say:
You got a song, man, sing it.
You got a bell, man, ring it.

You hurried off to Henry in his cell
before the trees could bring their flowers
back to Sleepy Hollow.
You sent your last letter months ago
about the poems you could not write,
no words to sing when the president swears
that God breathes the psalms of armies in his ear,
and flags twirl by the millions
to fascinate us like dogs at the dinner table.
You apologized for what you could not say,
as if the words were missing teeth
you searched for with your tongue,
and then a poem flashed across the page,
breaking news of music interrupting news of war:
You got a song, man, sing it.
You got a bell, man, ring it.

Today you died two thousand miles from Sleepy Hollow,
somewhere near the border with México, the territory
Thoreau wandered only in jailhouse sleep.
Your lungs folded their wings in a land of drought
and barbed wire, boxcars swaying intoxicated at 4 AM
and unexplained lights hovering in the desert.
You said: *There's a lot of places out there, friend,*
so you would go, smuggling a suitcase of words
across every border carved by the heel
of mapmakers or conquerors, because
you had an all-night conversation with the world,

hearing the beat of unsung poems in every voice,
visiting the haunted rooms in every face.
Drive, you said, because poets must
bring the news to the next town:
You got a song, man, sing it.
You got a bell, man, ring it.

THE FACE ON THE ENVELOPE

for Julia de Burgos (1914–1953)

Julia was tall, so tall, the whispers said,
the undertakers amputated her legs at the knee
to squeeze her body into the city coffin
for burial at Potter's Field.

Dead on a street in East Harlem:
She had no discharge papers
from Goldwater Memorial Hospital,
no letters from Puerto Rico, no poems.
Without her name, three words
like three pennies stolen from her purse
while she slept off the last bottle of rum,
Julia's coffin sailed to a harbor
where the dead stand in the rain
patient as forgotten umbrellas.

All her poems flowed river-blue, river-brown, river-red.
Her Río Grande de Loíza was a fallen blue piece of sky;
her river was a bloody stripe whenever the torrent
burst and the hills would vomit mud.

A monument rose at the cemetery in her hometown.
There were parks and schools. She was memorized.

Yet only the nameless, names plucked as their faces
turned away in labor or sleep, could return Julia's name to her
with the grace of a beggar offering back a stranger's wallet.

Years later, a nameless man from Puerto Rico,
jailed in a city called Hartford, would read her poem
about the great river of Loíza till the river gushed
through the faucet in his cell and sprayed his neck.
Slowly, every night, as fluorescent light grew weary
and threatened to quit, he would paint Julia's face
on an envelope: her hair in waves of black, her lips red,
her eyelids so delicate they almost trembled. Finally,
meticulous as a thief, he inscribed the words: *Julia de Burgos.*

He could never keep such treasure under his pillow,
so he slipped a letter into the envelope
and mailed it all away, flying through the dark
to find my astonished hands.

NOT WORDS BUT HANDS

for Yusef Komunyakaa

We have no words for you.

The poets hear the news,
this death unspeakable as the babble
of an auctioneer at the slave market.

There are no words in our language to say this.
We are singers who moan,
prophets with tongues missing
like the clappers of empty bells.

In your poems there are singers, prophets, slaves.
You hammered words for all of them.
But we have no words for you;
there is no name for the grief in your face.

We only have our hands, to soap your shirts
or ladle soup for you, grip your shoulder
or dim the lamp so you can sleep with visions
of the ball field by the lumber company
wars and wars ago.

And this, this poem,
this is my hand.

STONE HAMMERED TO GRAVEL

for poet Dennis Brutus, at eighty

The office workers did not know, plodding through 1963
and Marshall Square station in Johannesburg,
that you would dart down the street between them,
thinking the police would never fire into the crowd.
Sargeant Kleingeld did not know, as you escaped
his fumbling hands and the pistol on his hip,
that he would one day be a footnote in the book of your life.

The secret policeman on the corner did not know,
drilling a bullet in your back, that today the slug
would belong in a glass case at the museum of apartheid.
The bystanders did not know, as they watched
the coloured man writhing red on the ground,
that their shoes would skid in blood for years.

The ambulance men did not know,
when they folded the stretcher and refused you a ride
to the white hospital, that they would sit eternally
in hell's emergency room, boiling with a disease
that darkens their skin and leaves them screaming for soap.
The guards at Robben Island did not know,
when you hammered stone to gravel with Mandela,
that the South Africa of their fathers
would be stone hammered to gravel by the inmates,

who daydreamed a republic of the ballot
but could not urinate without a guard's permission.

Did you know?
When the bullet exploded the stars
in the cosmos of your body, did you know
that others would read manifestos by your light?
Did you know, after the white ambulance left,
before the coloured ambulance arrived, if you would live at all,
that you would banish the apartheid of the ambulance
with Mandela and a million demonstrators
dancing at every funeral?
Did you know, slamming the hammer into the rock's stoic face,
that a police state is nothing but a boulder
waiting for the alchemy of dust?
Did you know that, forty years later,
college presidents and professors of English
would raise their wine to your name
and wonder what poetry they could write
with a bullet in the back?

What do the people we call prophets know?
Can they conjure the world forty years from now?
Can the poets part the clouds for a vision in the sky
easily as sweeping curtains across the stage?

A beard is not the mark of prophecy
but the history of a man's face.

No angel shoved you into the crowd;
you ran because the blood racing to your heart
warned a prison grave would swallow you.
No oracle spread a banquet of vindication before you
in visions; you mailed your banned poems
cloaked as letters to your sister-in-law
because the silence of the world
was a storm flooding your ears.

South Africa knows. Never tell a poet: *Don't say that.*
Even as the guards watched you nodding in your cell,
even as you fingered the stitches fresh from the bullet,
the words throbbed inside your skull:
Sirens knuckles boots. Sirens knuckles boots.
Sirens knuckles boots.

RULES FOR CAPTAIN AHAB'S PROVINCETOWN POETRY WORKSHOP

1. Ye shall be free to write a poem on any subject, as long as it's the White Whale.

2. A gold doubloon shall be granted to the first among ye who in a poem sights the White Whale.

3. The Call Me Ishmael Award shall be given to the best poem about the White Whale, with publication in *The White Whale Review*.

4. The Herman Melville Memorial Picnic and Softball Game shall be open to whosoever of ye writes a poem about following thy Captain into the maw of hell to kill the White Whale.

5. There shall be a free floating coffin for any workshop participant who falls overboard whilst writing a poem about the White Whale.

6. There shall be a free leg, carved from the jawbone of a whale, for any workshop participant who is dismasted whilst writing a poem about the White Whale.

7. There shall be a free funeral at sea, complete with a chorus of stout hearties singing sea chanteys about the White Whale, for any workshop participant who is decapitated whilst writing a poem about the White Whale.

8. Ye who seek not the White Whale in thy poems shall be harpooned.

ADVICE TO YOUNG POETS

Never pretend
to be a unicorn
by sticking a plunger on your head

III

THE WEATHER-BEATEN FACE

RETURN

245 Wortman Avenue
East New York, Brooklyn

Forty years ago, I bled in this hallway.
Half-light dimmed the brick
like the angel of public housing.
That night I called and listened at every door:
In 1966, there was a war on television.

Blood leaked on the floor like oil from the engine of me.
Blood rushed through a crack in my scalp;
blood foamed in both hands; blood ruined my shoes.
The boy who fired the can off my head in the street
pumped what blood he could into his fleeing legs.
I banged on every door for help, spreading a plague
of bloody fingerprints all the way home to apartment 14F.

Forty years later, I stand in the hallway.
The dim angel of public housing is too exhausted
to welcome me. My hand presses
against the door at apartment 14F
like an octopus stuck to aquarium glass;
blood drums behind my ears.
Listen to every door: There is a war on television.

BLUES FOR THE SOLDIERS WHO TOLD YOU

I'm like a country who can't remember the last war.

—*Doug Anderson*

They told you that the enemy and the liberated throng
swaddle themselves in the same robes and rags,
wear the same masks with eyes that follow you,
pray in the same bewildering tongue, until your rifle
trembles to rake the faces at every checkpoint.
They told you about the corpse of a boy or girl
rolled at your feet, hair gray with the powder
of rubble and bombardment, flies a whirlpool blackening both eyes,
said you'll learn the words for apology too late to join
the ceremony, as flies become the chorus of your nightmares.
They told you about the double amputee from your town,
legs lopped off by the blast, his basketball friend
bumping home in a flag-draped coffin
the cameras will not film anymore,
about veterans who drench themselves in liquor
like monks pouring gasoline on their heads.

They told you in poems and stories
you did not read, or stopped reading
as your cheeks scorched with inexplicable fever,
and because they spoke with a clarity that burned your face,
because they saw with the vision of a telescope
revolving around the earth, they spent years wandering

through jails and bars, exiled to roads after midnight
where gas stations snap their lights off one by one,
seers unseen at the coffee shop waiting for bacon and eggs,
calling at 3 AM to say *I can't stop writing and you have to hear this.*
You will not hear this, even after the war is over
and the troops drown in a monsoon of desert flowers
tossed by the crowd, blooming in their mouths
to stop their tongues with the sweetness of it.

THE GOD OF THE WEATHER-BEATEN FACE

for Camilo Mejía, conscientious objector

The gods gathered:
the crusader god took off his helmet,
the desert warrior god stood his shield in the corner,
the sword-maker god sat between them sharpening blades,
the bombardier god spread his maps on the table,
the god who collects infidel heads traded trophies
with the god who collects heathen scalps,
the god of gold opened his handkerchief
for the god of oil to wipe his dripping chin,
the god who punishes sin with boils scratched his boils
and called the meeting to order.

And the gods said: *War.*

Sergeant Mejía heard the prisoner moan under the hood
as the guards shoved him into a steel closet, then pounded
with a sledgehammer on the door until the moaning stopped;
heard machine-gun fire slicing heads from necks
with a roar that would be the envy of swords;
heard a soldier sobbing in the toilet for the headless boy
who would open his eyes every time the soldier closed his own.

Sometimes a song drifts up
through the moaning and sledgehammers,

machine guns and sobbing.
Sometimes a voice floats above pandemonium
the way a seagull floats over burning ships.
Sergeant Mejía heard his father's song,
the peasant mass of Nicaragua:
Vos sos el Dios de los pobres,
el Dios humano y sencillo,
el Dios que suda en la calle,
el Dios de rostro curtido.
You are the God of the poor,
the human and simple God,
the God who sweats in the street,
the God of the weather-beaten face.

Iraq was crowded with the faces of this God.
They watched as Sergeant Mejía said *no* to the other gods,
miniscule word, a pebble, a grain of rice,
but the word flipped the table at the war council,
where the bombardier god had just dealt
the last hand to the god of oil,
and cards with dates of birth and death,
like tiny tombstones, fluttered away.
Sergeant no more, Camilo Mejía walked to jail.
Commanders fed the word *coward*
to the sniffing microphones of reporters
who repeated obediently: *coward.*

The cell crowded with faces too, unseen travelers
wandering in from a century of jails:
union organizer, hunger striker, freedom rider,
street corner agitator, conscientious objector.

The God of the weather-beaten face,
dressed as an inmate steering a mop,
smuggled in the key one day, and Camilo Mejía
walked with him through epiphany's gate.

BETWEEN THE ROCKETS AND THE SONGS

New Year's Eve, 2003

The fireworks began at midnight,
golden sparks and rockets hissing
through the confusion of trees above our house.
I would prove to my son, now twelve,
that there was no war in the sky, not here,
so we walked down the road
to find the place where the fireworks began.
We swatted branches from our eyes,
peering at a house where the golden blaze
dissolved in smoke. There was silence,
a world of ice, then voices rose up
with the last of the sparks, singing,
and when the song showered down on us
through the leaves we leaned closer, like trees.
Rockets and singing from the same house, said my son.
We turned back down the road,
at the end of the year, at the beginning of the year,
somewhere between the rockets and the songs.

To the Burmese Albino Python Living in the Next Room

I have seen the snapshot
of the other Burmese albino python
unspooled across the floor and up the wall,
measured at twenty feet
by the nervous little man in the picture.

I have seen the National Geographic special,
Pets That Eat Their Owners, starring
a Burmese python in Wisconsin.
The video shot by the cops wandered over beer cans
and pizza boxes before zooming into focus
on the sneakers of the snake enthusiast,
rolled in his snake like the shredded beef in a tortilla.
He forgot to wash his hands.

I have seen the Book of Snakes,
instructing me that one day
you will hunger for a whole frozen goat,
stuffed in a garbage bag
and defrosted in the bathtub.
The Book of Genesis calls you the Devil,
hissing in Eve's ear about the landlord of Eden.

My comrade the angry bald man,
who is unafraid of police
throwing nets over demonstrators,
will not sleep in the same room with you,
and neither will my father-in-law,
who laughs at explosions.
Our wise friends advise banishment
to the reptile house at the zoo;
our paranoid friends hand us lists of enemies
you should strangle in their sleep.

Yet you are so yellow, yellow
as the paint on a madman's brush,
yellow as the soul of a canary.
You amaze my fingertips, polished skin
far from the slime of your reputation,
as you glide by on your belly with eight hundred ribs,
investigate the world with a sniffing tongue.

Above all, I celebrate you because you eat rats,
the informer in the Garden of Eden
who spelled your name for God
even as rat armies massed to march across the earth:
plague-rats, grain-stealing rats, garbage-swollen rats,
ankle-ripping rats, night-hallucination rats,
Brooklyn-insomnia-with-a-baseball-bat rats.

Some pray for salvation to the same God who created rats;
others leave the bathtub filled to drown the rats at night.
You greet every rat with joy,
the S of your neck whipping the air,
jaws unhinged to gorge on rat head
and shoulders, then the feet
poking up in death's last embarrassment,
till only the tail is left,
hanging from your mouth
like a fine Cuban cigar.

WHY MY BONES HATE THE ICE

This is why my bones hate the ice:
Ten years ago I stumbled across that white mirror
and snapped my foot off.
I could hear the ankle in my boot
crunching like a mouthful of ice.
I rolled through traffic to the curb,
and the cars stopped, their drivers afraid
to crush a fender on the Bigfoot
flushed from hiding in the woods.
Later, my bones spoke to me
through morphine, the great translator:

That could have been your head,
another Mexican sugar skull
on the Day of the Dead
with your name scripted in red letters.
You are nothing but a Neanderthal
and this is the new Ice Age.
Your bones will stack up
with all the other bones
below the ice of ten thousand years.
Your foot is mummified, wrapped
for the voyage to the next world,
and your ancestors are waving their hats at you

from the shore in a country where ice does not exist,
calling to you the way your grandfather did:
Ven acá. Come here.

Now I need my cane to walk a trail in the woods.
The brook is frozen, braiding the light at noon,
and the black water pulses through cracks in white,
where the ice is a lost civilization of fountains and catacombs,
the fangs of saber-toothed tigers, a coral reef of glass.
That's why my bones love the ice.

THE CAVES OF CAMUY

for Katherine Gilbert-Espada

In the sleep of hysterectomy,
deep in the well where anesthesia
dropped you like a bucket
banging and spinning to oblivion,
you saw the old poet again.
You named your son for him,
Clemente for Clemente, but now
there would be no more sons or daughters,
your tide of blood burned away like the drought
at the end of the world, so you summoned this apparition
back from the place where mountains tend his grave
in secret, hoarding the stone of Clemente Soto Vélez.
The poet spoke a hieroglyphic tongue, yet you read
the pictures carved in air, understood the words he said:

Gather good brushes and good paper,
collect your colors and your rags.
Paint the caves of the river Camuy.
Paint the faces chanting in stone before the wind
presses a finger against their lips.
Paint the dripstone, flowstone, rimstone, limestone.
Paint the caverns where conquistadores and geologists
went mad hearing the echo of waterfalls they could never find.

Paint the blue crabs escaping your footsteps.
Paint the trilobites waking up hungry after millions of years.
Paint the bats fleeing the flashlight with panicky wings.
Paint my face squinting in the flashlight,
amazing the discoverers who swore they were first.
Paint my skin smooth again, like a boy
who leaps from the rock to the river.
Paint my white hair streaming in the chamber
they call the Hall of White Maidens.
Paint my black eyes hunting in the dark.
Paint so I can walk from the cemetery
to sit at the window of the house
where I was born a hundred years ago,
contemplating the Puerto Rican parakeet
extinct everywhere but the tree by my window.

Gather good brushes and good paper,
and the creatures in the caves will stir:
singers in the circle of the first maracas,
conquerors and geologists flinging their helmets,
crabs, bats, trilobites, parakeets, poets with white hair spilling,
your sons and daughters pouring from the mouth of the world.

Notes on the Poems

NOT HERE: "In the name of our love . . ." The fourth stanza quotes eight lines from the poem "Pastoral de Chile" (IX) by Raúl Zurita, translated by Jack Schmitt in *Anteparadise* (University of California Press, 1986). Salvador Allende was the democratically elected socialist president of Chile from 1970 to 1973. Allende's Popular Unity government was overthrown in a U. S.-backed military coup on September 11, 1973, and he died that day at La Moneda, the presidential palace, after giving his final radio address to the nation. The poem is based in part on a visit to La Moneda with Zurita in July, 2004.

SOMETHING ESCAPES THE BONFIRE: The first two sections rely on the account by Joan Jara in her book, *Víctor: An Unfinished Song* (Bloomsbury, 1998); the third section is based on a conversation with her at Estadio Víctor Jara in Santiago de Chile in July 2004. The first section quotes, in the original Spanish and the translation by Joan Jara, the song "Plegaria a un labrador" ("The Peasant's Prayer") by Víctor Jara, which appears on his recording *Pongo en tus manos abiertas . . .* (*I Put in Your Open Hands . . .*) (Warner Music Chile, 2001). The song "Venceremos" ("We Will Win"), referenced in the second section, was the anthem of the Popular Unity movement and the Allende government.

THE SOLDIERS IN THE GARDEN: The first two stanzas rely in part on the account by Adam Feinstein in his book, *Pablo Neruda: A Passion for Life* (Bloomsbury, 2004), and a visit to Isla Negra in July 2004.

BLACK ISLANDS: "Isla Negra," literally "Black Island," is a village—not an island—on the coast of central Chile, best known as the home of Pablo Neruda, who named the coastal area. Rubén Darío (1867–1916) was a major modernist poet of Nicaragua.

RAIN WITHOUT RAIN: "A human ear in the soup" and other details in the third stanza come from the indictment brought by Judge Baltasar Garzón of Spain against General Augusto Pinochet, cited by Ariel Dorfman in *Exorcising Terror: The Incredible Unending Trial of General Augusto Pinochet* (Seven Stories Press, 2002). The last line comes from "Poema 20" of the *Veinte poemas de amor y una canción desesperada (Twenty Love Poems and a Song of Despair)* (Nascimiento, 1924) by Pablo Neruda.

NOT PAINT AND WOOD: "I want to climb the steps / at Macchu Picchu" refers to the ruins of an Inca city in the Andean highlands of Péru, made famous by Pablo Neruda's epic poem, *Alturas de Macchu Picchu (Heights of Macchu Picchu)*. "He likes for me to be still" refers to a line in "Poema 15" of the *Veinte poemas de amor y una canción desesperada (Twenty Love Poems and a Song of Despair)* (Nascimiento, 1924) by Neruda.

CITY OF GLASS: "La Chascona" refers to a woman with tangled or messy hair. This is a reference to Matilde Urrutia, and the name of the house built by Pablo Neruda for his future wife in Santiago de Chile in 1952. Today the restored house is the headquarters of the Fundación Neruda.

AN ADMIRER OF GENERAL PINOCHET . . . : This poem is based on excerpts from birthday messages and other testimonials to General Augusto Pinochet found on the Web site of the Fundación

Pinochet, translated by Martín Espada. The title alludes to a poem by Ernesto Cardenal entitled "Somoza desveliza la estatua de Somoza en el estadio Somoza" ("Somoza Unveils Somoza's Statue of Somoza in the Somoza Stadium"), translated by Donald Walsh.

GENERAL PINOCHET AT THE BOOKSTORE: This poem relies in part on a report published on the Web site of Radio Cooperativa, Santiago de Chile, July 2, 2004.

YOU GOT A SONG, MAN: "You got a song, man, sing it . . ." The end of each stanza quotes two lines from a poem by Robert Creeley, "Old Story," which appeared in *Ploughshares,* Vol. 31, No. 1, Spring 2005, edited by Martín Espada. The first stanza is based on a visit with Creeley to Sleepy Hollow Cemetery in Concord, Massachusetts, in April, 2004.

THE FACE ON THE ENVELOPE: "river-blue, river-brown, river-red . . ." The third stanza paraphrases four lines from the poem "Río Grande de Loíza" by Julia de Burgos, translated by Jack Agüeros in *Song of the Simple Truth: The Complete Poems* of Julia de Burgos (Curbstone Press, 1997). The first stanza relies on the account in the introductory essay by Agüeros. The Río Grande de Loíza is a river in northeastern Puerto Rico.

STONE HAMMERED TO GRAVEL: "Sirens knuckles boots . . ." The end of the poem refers to the title of the first poetry collection by Dennis Brutus, entitled *Sirens Knuckles Boots* (Mbari Publications, 1963). The first three stanzas of the poem rely in part on the account by Craig W. McLuckie, "A Biographical Introduction to Dennis Brutus' Art and Activism" in *Critical Perspectives on Dennis Brutus* (Three Continents Press, 1995).

BLUES FOR THE SOLDIERS WHO TOLD YOU: "I'm like a country who can't remember the last war . . ." The epigraph is from the poem "Blues," by Doug Anderson. In the first stanza, "the corpse of a boy or girl / rolled at your feet" refers to Anderson's poem "Xin Loi." Both poems appear in Anderson's book, *The Moon Reflected Fire* (Alice James Books, 1994). In the same stanza, "a whirlpool blackening both eyes" refers to a poem by George Evans entitled "Two Girls," from *The New World* (Curbstone Press, 2002).

THE GOD OF THE WEATHER-BEATEN FACE: "Vos sos el Dios de los pobres . . ." The fourth stanza quotes four lines from the song cycle called the "Misa Campesina Nicaragüense" ("Nicaraguan Peasant Mass") by Carlos Mejía Godoy, translated by Martín Espada. A well-known singer and composer in Nicaragua, Carlos Mejía Godoy is the father of Camilo Mejía.

THE CAVES OF CAMUY: The Río Camuy is a river in northwestern Puerto Rico that runs underground for five miles, and is home to an enormous system of caves. Certain details in the second stanza are based on the account by Russell and Jeanne Gurnee in *Discovery at the Río Camuy* (Crown Publishers, 1974). The poem also refers to Clemente Soto Vélez (1905–1993), a major Puerto Rican poet and leader of the independence movement who was born in Lares, not far from Camuy. Soto Vélez was a close friend of the author and his wife, who named their son for him.

Biographical Note

Martín Espada was born in Brooklyn, New York, in 1957. He has published thirteen books in all as a poet, essayist, editor, and translator. His last collection of poems, *Alabanza: New and Selected Poems (1982–2002)*, was published by Norton in 2003, received the Paterson Award for Sustained Literary Achievement, and was named an American Library Association Notable Book of the year. An earlier collection, *Imagine the Angels of Bread* (Norton, 1996), won an American Book Award and was a finalist for the National Book Critics Circle Award. Other books of poetry include *A Mayan Astronomer in Hell's Kitchen* (Norton, 2000), *City of Coughing and Dead Radiators* (Norton, 1993), and *Rebellion is the Circle of a Lover's Hands* (Curbstone, 1990). He has received numerous awards, including the Robert Creeley Award, the Antonia Pantoja Award, a Gustavus Myers Outstanding Book Award, the Paterson Poetry Prize, the Charity Randall Citation, a Guggenheim Foundation Fellowship, the PEN/Revson Fellowship, and two NEA Fellowships. His poems have appeared in *The New Yorker*, *The New York Times Book Review*, *Harper's*, *The Nation*, and *The Best American Poetry*. He has also published a collection of essays, *Zapata's Disciple* (South End, 1998); edited two anthologies, *Poetry Like Bread: Poets of the Political Imagination from Curbstone Press* (Curbstone, 1994) and *El Coro: A Chorus of Latino and Latina Poetry* (University of Massachusetts, 1997); and released an audiobook of poetry called *Now the Dead will Dance the Mambo* (Leapfrog, 2004). Espada is a professor in the Department of English at the University of Massachusetts–Amherst, where he teaches creative writing and the work of Pablo Neruda.